Bargain with Ease

Indispensable Bargaining Steps Set Into Practice

by John A. Sarette

Copyright © 2018 by John A. Sarette

All rights reserved.

ISBN-13: 978-1986345422

DEDICATION

To my wife, Presely. I'm so thankful for your encouragement and help in getting this book written.

CONTENTS

Acknowledgments i
Introduction 1
Research 5
Communication 9
Negotiating Authority 15
Profit 21
Walking Away 27
Practice 31
Putting It All Together 35

ACKNOWLEDGMENTS

Thank you Dianne Chapman McCleery, my wonderful editor. And thank you Danae Little, a marvelous writer who also happens to teach publishing. I also thank the group of writers in Danae's workshop for the many ideas and tips as we turned our manuscripts and material into published works.

INTRODUCTION

Who likes paying retail? I don't, and you should not either. So let's stop buying products and services using the rules written by slick marketing firms, highly geared to extract the most dollars they can get from the average consumer.

This book will reveal the five necessary steps to guide you in paying less for products and services in the retail marketplace and specialty shops, as well as in paying much, much less for goods and services in secondary markets. This system is also a go-to for negotiating new and used car purchases, at swap meets, on craigslist, and the list goes on and on! You will explore the system in enough detail and develop a straightforward path, time tested, in the "Win-Win" fashion. You will realize lowered prices, keeping more money in your pockets, while also winning the trust and respect of the retailers and sellers with whom you are doing business!

"Does this mean that you can get a discount even

from major retailers such as Wal-Mart and Costco?" Absolutely, as you will see in examples laid out in the readings of those specific occurrences. The examples go hand in hand with both the thought processes and steps necessary in aligning your interests in keeping your hard earned money, along with the interests of the retailers in making a profit.

"How about every day purchases such as my morning cafe mocha latte?" "How about when I'm buying groceries and other staples at any of the supermarket retailers in my neighborhood?" It is up to you to decide where and how you want to spend your energy and time in saving your precious resources and in keeping dollars in your bank account, and out of theirs.

Every purchase is open to negotiation. Where and why you choose to seek lower prices, as well as win influence with your trading partner, will become keenly apparent. As you practice and exercise these five steps and adhere to the principles in the open marketplaces during your travels to local shops and beyond, you will transition from a novice to an expert bargainer.

The negotiation framework entails five indispensible essentials. Success is determined not whether or not you make the purchase or enter into a contract, but rather how well you implement the process. You will discover the details to increase both your bottom line financially as well as improving your buyer-seller relationships.

The five steps to remember are simply:
- 1 - Research
- 2 - Communication
- 3 - Negotiating Authority
- 4 - Profit
- 5 - Walking Away

You will explore each of the five steps in detail in the following chapters. The information and examples provided demonstrate that all purchases are open to negotiation. Work the five steps in the framework and start your savings!

CHAPTER 1

RESEARCH

Do your research, do your homework, and develop a knowledge base on the products, items, and services that you will be negotiating.

The internet and printed media are jam packed with almost any detail required of any single item or service that has ever been sold. In stating the obvious, that is a great place to start your research, your homework. For almost any item that can be purchased today, not only are descriptions, weight, features, and specifications compiled and contrasted, but also available are databases of customers reviews that can aid the quest in your search for the best products for the money. Video channels also allow a researcher to observe a product in use as seen through the camera lens of other purchasers and reviewers.

When purchasing items for hobbies, a great deal of examination goes into all aspects of these purchases. People love their hobbies! When the hobby involves an organized group, members have an incredible wealth of knowledge and inclination to help others achieve the same entertainment and satisfaction that they have derived from their hobby. Tap into this vast knowledge when conducting your research.

Your review should not begin and end at the internet, media, and hobby groups. Sales staff who are selling the products and services can be an enormous resource and tremendous help as you sift through the multitudes of options that are under consideration.

I had spent six months looking for a used 1997 BMW 840CI sports coupe, the final year that the model had been imported into the United States. I had conducted a detailed review of the 8 series and liked the aspects of a sports coupe that were found in that particular model. Now to find one, the right one at the right price! There are websites devoted to almost every car imaginable, and the 8 series was no exception. My research was easily accomplished using the internet.

The exact year, model, color, and optioned vehicle that I desired was located after this patient search. The seller was then contacted, first by a text message and then via phone conversation. He lived in a city about 100 miles away and had listed the car for twelve thousand dollars. We talked about the car and in our exchanges, I impressed on him that I was a serious buyer and was exceedingly familiar with the particulars of the car he was selling. With an informed approach to the purchase, I presented my position on what I was willing to offer him for the vehicle.

I had found several other BMW 8 series advertised in his area. Most of these were listed for sale in the twelve to twenty thousand dollar range like his. I stated to the seller that these cars "languished in the used car marketplace," and that when an 8 series was priced in the seven to eight thousand dollar range, that car would sell. He listened, agreed that he could move off the advertised price, and asked what I was willing to pay. I offered seven thousand five hundred dollars, and added that a previously listed 840CI had recently sold in that ball park. He thought about the offer for a little bit and agreed that he could sell the car to me for seventy-five hundred dollars, on the stipulation that I would not ask for an even lower price upon vehicle inspection. The price was agreed upon with the caveat that I could walk away from the deal should inspections or a test ride fail to impress.

I spoke with a mechanic that worked on the car before arriving for the test ride. Everything was up to snuff according to the mechanic's report, and the test ride showed no deficiencies. The vehicle performance was also to my liking, so I purchased the car. The results of my research and thoughtful presentation to the seller resulted in a forty-five hundred dollar savings!

It is important in the bargaining strategy to get the ball rolling in the right direction. This is accomplished in the research step. Do your homework and develop a thorough knowledge base of the item under consideration to include price and value. Find out what others have paid for the item and determine its value to you. With knowledge, you have the proper ammunition to drive the deal forward.

CHAPTER 2

COMMUNICATION

Normal tone and mannerism drive our message when engaging the sales force.

Experts agree that communication skills are critical to how effective you are in your professional and personal life. This is a crucial element as well in your negotiating strategies. Although many experts would point out that the focus is on the content of your message, I would say the tone and gestures are just as important. Use normal tone and mannerisms when engaging the sales force.

Great late-night radio hosts would be my companions when taking long trips at night across my home state of California, including two to three hour trips to San Francisco and longer trips down to Southern California. What kept me engaged and awake was not the content of some of the shows (discussions of UFO sightings across the Southwest or an occasional alien abduction revelation), but the radio personality's tone and inflections.

How you sound when you tell your story can be more important than the story itself. In fact, "One of the most compelling sounds for the human ear is the sound of another human voice," says David Candow, a voice coach for some of National Public Radio's most well-known hosts since 1995. Some Radio hosts often speak loudly and with a lot of hype to get attention. They are looking for an emotional response from their listeners, and they often use volume, pitch, and tone to get it. But unlike those loud, brash talk show hosts, those tones and sounds probably won't work for us—particularly when it comes to negotiating for products and services. Bargaining requires a more conversational, authentic, and normal tone.

Much is written about negotiation strategy, and Keld Jensen in a blog details some thoughtful steps you can utilize in setting your tone and manner. The negotiation must find a cooperative solution, and both parties will need to feel satisfied in the communication process. Before the real negotiations even start, a proper engagement of both parties must be developed to open a receptive channel for the negotiation. This opens a degree of trust with one another and a favorable communication climate to start the bargaining process.

The opening is often the crucial step that sets the

stage for the rest of the bargaining process. This cannot be stressed enough! The atmosphere and the tone in which you present your argument can mean more to the transaction than any other matter. Having the ear of an engaged listener gets the negotiation off to a successful start.

Your first step in engaging a negotiating partner is to become acquainted with the other party. This may have to happen quickly in a retail setting when sales staff are busy. On the other hand, you may be afforded some luxury of time depending on the purchase and/or a less hectic sales setting. It is not a good step to enter a shop and start asking for discounts without proper engagement.

I was shopping with a friend at a country and western clothing store. After picking out an expensive pair of boots, my friend took the boots over to the somewhat busy sales counter and immediately asked if they could discount the item. The sales associate at the counter appeared somewhat taken aback by this direct approach. The answer on the discount was no, with an added comment of that particular item not being on sale, but that there was a clearance rack in the back of the store.

What went wrong? Well, my friend had not taken any time with the associate to develop a level of familiarity and trust. A merchant should feel at ease in a conversation when a request for a discount is broached. A better approach could have been in asking for the help of the associate in looking at their line of boots, to gain some trust and rapport between the parties. Then a discussion on movement of the price could have been started.

The following example illustrates what can happen when you develop a dynamic with your sales counterpart. A few years ago I happened to have the weekend off from some work that I was doing in Germany and had the opportunity to take a trip to Paris along with my wife. While making our way through the hustle and bustle in the St. Germaine restaurant section, a barker was hawking up business to his eatery. "Hey, what part of the States are you from," he directed towards me. "Whoa," I thought, "is it written all over me?" My wife and I paused, and we got into a pleasant conversation with the guy. He told me that he had lived in Boston for years before settling in France. I related that I had New England origins and had grown up about fifty miles from Boston. He invited us into the restaurant; we accepted and ordered full-priced meals. Then I heard the phrase "Carte Blanche," spoken in real French for the first time as my new friend directed our waiter to bring drinks, escargot, and later chocolate profiteroles!

We had quickly developed a personal chemistry that led to carte blanche (that is on-the-house in English) beverages, snails, and dessert. His largesse was based on our conversational dynamic rather than the restaurant's bottom line. Without even asking, our dining experience had been discounted based on the tone and trust from our initial conversation!

When you are ready to move forward after getting acquainted, take the opportunity to hesitate or fall silent, forcing the other party to start talking. In doing this, you will obtain more, often valuable information. Cooperation is a dominant theme, be reasonable and polite.

When I needed to purchase a laptop computer, I visited online resources and focused my search for a reasonably priced model. I made a trip to a local Costco and toured the display area for a reasonable match. A particular "display model only" sign on one of the units caught my attention. It had all of the features that were required and had been already discounted by the store, as evidenced by the ninety-seven cent price ending. I wondered if there was any price movement left, so I asked for assistance from an associate whose badge identified him as a supervisor. I asked him about a couple of differences in similarly priced models, and he told me the pros and cons of the units. He did recommend the "display model unit" as one that should be given high consideration. I agreed that I might get that one and took that opportunity to ask if there was any price movement left since it was the not only a display model, but also the only one left in stock.

I broached this question in a normal tone and in an unhurried pace, and then fell silent in wait for his response. Although we had only just met and conversed briefly, I sensed that we were both at ease in our conversation and negotiation. The supervisor stated that there was that possibility and that he would consult the manager. He left along with the display unit's identification tag and with the promise to "be right back."

In about five minutes, the supervisor returned with the tag which had an additional $150 discount subtracted from the sales price, signed by a store manager. I agreed to the purchase, and the supervisor said that the laptop and accessories could be picked up at the cage once the rest of my shopping was completed. He then handed me the discounted unit tag to give to a cashier and went on his way.

Use normal tone and mannerism to lay the groundwork for bargaining, and you will drive the course to a successful conclusion of the interaction. Although each of the five steps are important in the bargaining process, the communication piece is under our immediate control. It is to be practiced, evaluated, and improved upon.

CHAPTER 3

NEGOTIATING AUTHORITY

You must negotiate with someone that has the authority to negotiate, or with someone who will advocate your stated position to those with decision making authority.

It is not that often, since we live on opposite sides of the country, that I get some time to spend with my brother. He runs a successful automotive repair shop, and deals with customers and employees day in and day out. You are often dealing with these successful small business entrepreneurs in many of the business establishments that you frequent. From the dry cleaners, hairdresser boutiques, restaurants, coffee shops, gas stations, convenience stores, etc., it is almost too easy to recognize the owner/operator. They are aware and engaged!

When my brother and I do get together, our conversations are light and easy as we reminisce the past, look to the future, and live in the now. We had met up at a wedding held in Austin, Texas. While out to eat on the day after the wedding, we passed through a franchised food establishment where he pointed out categories of the employees working there in a way that should be considered in your negotiations.

One group comprised those employees who are engaged and attentive. Those on the way up and those stable in their positions, possibly content to work at the establishment for years. The other group held the less attentive and less engaged employees.

This was a busy food establishment, and there was not time for any negotiations. However, which group of team members would you seek out for a negotiation interaction?

It is imperative that you find an employee from the first group, the engaged and attentive group. These employees are more likely to have authority to make decisions. If not, they still might advocate your position to the decision makers (sometimes it takes your encouragement). When you are confronted with several employees at a business and you have to make a choice, address as much of the group as possible while asking for assistance. The engaged, attentive employee will typically step up.

With about three hours to spare before having to be back at the airport for our trip to California, we took the time and hustled to a world-famous BBQ establishment just outside of Austin in the town of Driftwood. We wanted to take their offerings with us on the airplane to share with our friends back home.

I spoke a general question to the staff who were taking orders about our plans to hand carry the BBQ on the airplane, and that we would be sharing it with our friends back in California. An engaging and attentive cashier latched onto my request for suggestions of what would travel well. I heeded her advice and placed an order of what was recommended. She assured us that the take-out would be well packaged for carrying half way across the country. She was not only engaging and attentive, but seemed to be an employee that could make a decision.

While paying for the order and maintaining casual conversation, I asked which bottled BBQ sauce should we purchase with the order. She reached up onto the wall and took down bottles of the two sauce flavors they carried. Even though they were listed at $9 dollars per bottle, she stated that there would be no charge. We were working with a decision maker! I thanked her for the extras and ordered a ball cap with the BBQ establishment logo that I had been eyeing, as well as a couple of Tee shirts for my mother-in-law and for my niece. Making the customer happy can also result in more sales for the establishment.

Another case in point occurred when I purchased

a high-end metal detector for use in my gold prospecting hobby. I had been interested in purchasing a good metal detector and had located a retailer in the foothills about thirty-five miles from my home. I took a trip out to the shop and found that they did have a detector that would suit my purpose. However it was an older model unit, "new old stock," as it is called in the business. The original hobbyist business owner was no longer running the shop. As I discovered, the new owner was slowly selling off the remaining stock, and the business location was transitioning to a different enterprise.

The sales clerk discussed the merits of the detector that I was interested in. He was asked if we could negotiate the price of that equipment since all sales were final on the remaining stock. He stated that he did not have authority on pricing other than what was marked, but would relay an offer to the new owner. He added that the new owner was indisposed at the moment, so he would have to get back to me later in the week. A solid offer was made for the sales clerk to relay based on the fact that an upgraded detector was now available from the manufacturer and that this was a final sale.

As promised, I received a call from the sales clerk later in the week. The owner had countered my original offer, which was close enough for me to accept. Another trip to the store was made to complete the sales transaction. Six hundred dollars was saved from the original price. I was happy to have my new toy, and the business was happy to have reduced their stock in gold prospecting equipment.

When you enter a business establishment, pay attention to the associates involved in the operation. Look for those who have the propensity to engage in product discussions. Look for those with decision authority and those who will advocate your position to the decision makers.

CHAPTER 4

PROFIT

You must allow and factor for the business or person that you are dealing with to make a profit and/or have a gain through the transaction.

There can be a multitude of reasons that a business exists, and you can make the point that a business exists to make a profit. Simple enough for your purpose, you have to remember when negotiating that the other party has a bottom line. And the bottom line is a return on their investment, the profit.

This fact is in lock step with the first rule in persuading arguments, that you have to do your homework! In the new and used automobile buying business, dealers know exactly how that new or used gem of a car should be priced, as well as some step-wise negotiated discount percentages to offer in order to arrive at a completed contract with the consumer. Large purchase negotiations in this industry are broad, extensive, and too much to cover adequately here. But suffice to say that the willingness to work the five steps of the system will go a long way to the buyer driving home their discounted, shiny next vehicle with the seller receiving a satisfactory return on their investment.

In discussing negotiating strategies with a friend of mine, we talked of some of the major purchases made in the past year for his arborist business. He incorporates the strategies discussed in these pages.

He recently purchased a new, forty-one foot Fifth Wheel recreational vehicle. His business takes him throughout Northern and Central California. A project might see him spending several weeks away from home as he travels throughout California, including Yosemite National Park and along the roadways from Redding to Bakersfield. Underestimated lodging expenses had taken a toll on his company's bottom line. The Fifth Wheel could be the purchase needed for him to keep his project bids competitive, while still affording his company a year-end profit.

Armed with the knowledge of a nationwide research of RV models, he attended a late season Camping and Recreational Vehicle show at the local area Convention Center. Research (detailed in our first step) is a crucial and necessary step before ever entering into a sale negotiation, especially with the sophistication in which vehicle sales are conducted.

The data showed that his particular model RV had sold in other parts of the country in the fifty thousand dollar price range. What inference could be made from this knowledge? That those companies selling at that range would still turn a profit. Remember, from our simplified understandings, that a business exists to make a profit. His particular unit at the show had a retail price of one hundred and thirty thousand dollars, but had excitingly been reduced for the end-of-season show to that of only seventy-nine thousand dollars. What a bargain!

The slick sales agent attempted to obfuscate the negotiation with an issue of credit standing, but my savvy friend assured the agent that was of no concern. If his credit was not up to snuff, he would add five thousand dollars to any sales agreement and pay cash for the purchase. This led to the nuts and bolts of the deal, the offer. A fifty thousand dollar purchase price was offered, along with the additional amounts for RV treatments, several upgraded features, and applicable sales taxes. The out-the-door price offer totaled to just over sixty thousand dollars. The agent and his manager huddled for some time and then accepted the offer.

With both parties secure in the negotiated sales price, the contract was amicably written and executed. The important lesson of this step is that the RV dealer had negotiating room and would come out of the negotiation with a profit. Otherwise, the deal would not have been struck.

Also, my friend had saved over twenty-nine thousand dollars. Both parties were happy, the Arborist with the purchase and savings and the RV dealer with the sale and profit.

Another example of seller consideration occurred during an outing to a sportsmen's exposition, where hundreds of guides and merchants gather to sell their services and wares. I approached a display booth loaded with synthetic base-layer clothing and struck up a conversation with a salesperson who also happened be the owner of the clothing company. I asked him about his line of base wear clothing, particularly about the material and construction. I was particularly interested in Beanie caps that were available for five dollars each, having recently paid twenty-nine dollars for a similar cap from a different manufacturer.

I picked up a couple of the caps and asked if he could go eight bucks for the two. He replied that he had a slim profit margin and that five dollars each was a good price. I shook my head positively and agreed. "How do you make any money on these at all," I asked. I also mentioned that I had just paid twenty-nine dollars for an almost identical cap. His candid reply surprised me when he stated that each cap cost him two dollars to produce. He cut the material himself and had independent tailors construct the garments, who got paid per piece. I happily paid ten dollars for the Beanies.

You do have to consider the other party when

bargaining. They are entitled to a profit or other consideration in your negotiation; otherwise there is no need for them to be in business. Work at getting value and right pricing in the deal, but remain cognizant of your trading partner's position as well.

CHAPTER 5

WALKING AWAY

You must mentally prepare and be prepared to walk away.

   Preparation and the right mindset are necessary before you enter into any purchase situation. A prepared plan has to include the scenario where you "walk away" from the deal! It is important to emphasize that the buyer has tremendous leverage in the negotiation, especially a serious, informed buyer who is willing to walk away.
   I shopped with my wife for over eight hours at an outlet mall last year, looking for a particular style purse. We travelled from one designer store to the next. At one store, she found and had semi-settled on a purse that might fit the bill, a cross-body, messenger-type bag. I had struck up informative conversations with both the sales associate and the

manager of the establishment. Our conversations had been polite and cordial as my wife inspected the purse. I asked but could not get them to budge just a little off the standard 40 percent discount afforded to all shoppers.

The manager did offer to put the purse away for two days in case we did decide on getting it later. Even though the transaction did not occur, there were absolutely no hard feelings by either party when we walked away from the purchase. In analysis, perhaps there was not enough profit in that sale item for the company, so they held their ground. I learned a lesson as a buyer in that outlet designer shops might not be open to continued reductions in price until approved from the higher corporate chain. We did find a purse at another outlet shop, which my wife said was actually the purse she had wanted all along!

If you are not prepared to walk away from the deal, you could still implement strategies to try and lower costs for goods and services, but it not as easily done. A particular example of not having the ability to walk away occurs frequently in group situations of two and more.

During a vacation on the beautiful island of Boracay in the Philippines, a group of seven of us decided to partake in an off-road motorsport adventure that traveled from a concession park to the tallest mountain on the island. The group got way ahead of themselves and of my bargaining abilities as they were fitting on safety helmets and selecting the quad runners that they would be riding even before filling out the liability forms and making the payments. These tourist dependent operations are unusually conducive to bargaining and making some deals to just get you into their establishments and in the spending mode. But, having six of the seven person group already showing that money was no object, I had little recourse but to pay the full fare for our adventure. The trip vendor perceived my incapability of walking away. On a saving note, since I did ask for a group discount before payment and was told no, the cashier did include a little bonus for me. A free picture taken with a giant lizard up on my shoulders and wrapped around my neck. There was usually a 100 peso (about two US dollars) charge for that!

It can be tough to walk away from that "must have" next purchase, whether it be a fairly inexpensive deal on a new pair of shoes or on the high dollar car we've been drooling over at the dealer's lot. This step is as important as any of the previous steps in the system and the one that you need to rehearse before entering into the negotiation. You must have a bottom line and be willing to walk away. Visualize your way out.

When it comes time, avoid a dramatic exit. Take a step back and set the clear intention that you are no longer interested in the product at the price. The business owner or sales associate has taken the time to entertain your offer, and you want to be gracious with them. This also makes it easier for you to walk away.

CHAPTER 6

PRACTICE

Practice makes perfect and improvement examples.

You can get going with the bargaining system that has been presented in this publication. Practice makes sense in all endeavors, makes perfect, and can be rewarded with money savings your first time out.

I tagged along with my friends as they were shopping for gifts during the Christmas season. We were in a really nice boutique in the quaint foothill town of Sutter Creek, California. As my friends were putting in a serious shopping effort, I engaged one of the clerks in some light chit-chat, thanking them for the free cookies and coffee they had available for the shoppers. I happened to ask a couple of questions about the higher-end wool shirts that they carried. As we engaged in relaxed discussions about the benefits of wool over synthetics, I asked if there was any kind of sale coming up on that particular clothing line. I had not directly asked for a discount with the stated promise to buy should they offer; I was just gathering information about the product and the establishment concerning pricing. I was also keeping my negotiating level and energy focused and sharp. It sounds like a lot of work and maybe an embarrassing pain to keep up, but it is really not! It is just having a casual conversation with a merchant.

On another occasion, I had joined the back of the donut line after church one fine Sunday morning and right there it hit me. Let me see if I could get a volunteer parishioner to give some kind of discount on a donut. If you are going to use the system, you have to practice.

I was next in line to be served when Juanita, who I hadn't ever met, politely asked what type of donut that I wanted. In return I politely asked her what were available; we were having a fine initial conversation. When she had finished listing the donuts, I then asked her which ones might be available on a two for the price of one basis. The first thing she said was "You're kidding, right? You know this is a fund raiser!" Well, since I had engagement, the negotiations were on.

I explained in a normal tone that I was indeed serious. Since I was one of the last persons in line and there were still plenty of donuts left, the two-for-one pricing seemed like it might work for us. Then I added that if that wouldn't work, maybe I

Bargain With Ease

could buy one donut for half price. When retelling this occurrence and circumstances to my son and daughter-in-law, who were very attentive and interested in these bargaining steps, my son was quick to point out that maybe Juanita didn't have the authority to discount my donut. I might have had to go above and ask to see the priest for the discount!

Juanita looked me up and down and decided that she would grant me a two-for-one special. Then I asked her if I could get a cup of coffee included for that price as well. She shook her head and quickly stated that the coffee was free. At this point both of us were chuckling at the situation of our interactions. I paid with a five-dollar bill and told her to keep the change, as it really was a donation to one of the ministries of the church. Juanita to this day acknowledges me with the endearing call of "here comes my haggler."

With practice, you will get better and better at utilizing the bargaining framework. Seek engagement with sales associates when you shop, and begin to notice when you might bring up the idea of price movement of goods and services under consideration.

CHAPTER 7

PUTTING IT ALL TOGETHER

Sometimes buying situations bring opportunities where we can inquire about a discount. You might find that opportunity in a clearance isle or at an end of season blow-out sale. Sometimes you are just at the right place at the right time. Look to bargain when a situation ripe for negotiating materializes.

I had decided that I was going to get a television set for my mother-in-law on her birthday. Heading to the nearest Wal-Mart, I started looking through the myriad of sizes, features, and options available. A departmental sales associate was located and requested to explain the differences in a couple of the models. Having described the birthday celebrant's requirement for an easy-to-use model, I asked the associate what would be their recommendation.

He had demonstrated two models, same

manufacturer, with one having a price point of about fifty dollars above that of the lesser model. He highly recommended the lower priced unit due to its robust features and near comparison to its higher priced relative. I was happy with his knowledge and explanations and gave the okay for the purchase.

After the associate had spent five minutes giving a glowing review of the lesser priced model, he went to the back of the store to retrieve the TV from stock. He returned fairly quickly and stated that, much to his dismay, they were out of stock of that particular unit. He apologized for taking all of the time to sell me on that particular model TV and right after the decision was made to purchase, having to tell me, "Sorry, we are sold out of those."

It just so happened that the higher-priced TV had all of the same features, along with a couple not available on the lesser model. They did have that unit in stock and ready for immediate sale. I had earlier let the associate know my budget for the gift, and the in stock TV unit was over what I was willing to spend. I asked for a discount on the higher-end model.

He told me that he did not have authority to discount anything. If I'd like, he would call the electronics department manager, who did have the authority to offer discounts. "Sure, let's call him over," I agreed.

The department manager appeared shortly, and the sales associate provided the background assessment. Both he and I advocated my position in asking for a price adjustment on the available television set. The manager took a little time to verify inventories and item pricing, and offered me the brand new, higher-end model at a price below that of the lower-end unit. He sold me the TV for two hundred and eighty-nine dollars, a full eighty dollars off the original three hundred and sixty-nine dollar price. This was thirty dollars less than the three hundred and nineteen dollars I had been willing to pay for the lower-end model. I was happy with this turn of events and noted that there was still some profit in the item even at the discounted price.

In concluding a review, each of the five-steps of the bargaining system were travelled in completing this transaction, from the initial review of TV models and pricing to the engaged communication style with sales staff. We then continued in the system to negotiate with the department manager, who had the authority to make a price-point adjustment. Even though our initial discussions were with an associate that did not have decision making authority, he paved the way to introducing us to the decision maker. In the final analysis, we did not inject a pricing demand in the negotiation, but really had inferred that we would pay the price of the lesser model for the higher-end model. The price point selected by the manager is almost inconsequential to the outcome. We purchased the gift at a price we thought was fair given the underlying criteria for the purchase. Otherwise, we had been primed to walk away from the transaction to seek a purchase at another establishment. We received value and savings, and the department left the transaction with both a satisfied customer and a profit.

It is clear that there are a multitude of opportunities where a discount on price for goods or service may be reasonable. Determine what an item or service is worth to you and bargain for the price where you are happy. You do not have to and probably should not haggle over insignificant amounts. When you have engaged a deal-maker and have the other steps of the process covered, go ahead and ask for a discount or potential price movement.

Bargaining is the age-old tradition of "getting to the final price." And when you reach that price, agree to the purchase and stop negotiating. Light chit-chat at this point is okay, but steer any continued conversation away from the deal, politics, or religion. You do not want the deal to unravel.

Bargaining has worked for centuries, and will work for you. Start using this indispensible five-step system and you will be on your way to getting your bargain with ease!

NOTES

1. Lisa B. Marshall, "Do You Have a Radio Voice?" Quickanddirtytips.com, July 26, 2013, http://www.quickanddirtytips.com/business-career/communication/do-you-have-a-radio-voice

2. Keld Jensen, "How to Open a Negotiation," Wordpress, November 2, 2010, https://keldjensen.wordpress.com/2010/11/02/how-to-open-a-negotiation

ABOUT THE AUTHOR

John Sarette grew up in a small New England town. He has made his home in Northern California for the last twenty-five years and enjoys the recreational opportunities abundant in the foothills and mountains of the Sierras.

https://www.facebook.com/JohnASaretteAuthor

www.ingramcontent.com/pod-product-compliance
Lightning Source LLC
Chambersburg PA
CBHW030054230526
45471CB00003B/1098